GUIDE TO MAKING SMART DECISIONS:
14 Smart ways of making fearless decisions in every area of life.

Pedro D. Jackson

Table of content

Chapter 1

RECOGNIZE GOALS AND DESIRED OUTCOME.

Objectives and Desired Outcomes
Having picked the needs you need to address, you are currently prepared to become more unambiguous about your objectives and wanted results for the number of inhabitants in the center. Clear objectives and wanted results are significant for knowing where you are going, ensuring all accomplices are in total agreement, zeroing in on endeavors on what is generally critical, and estimating your effect.

Why distinguish objectives and results?
Clear objectives and results will assist you with choosing the most suitable methods or cycles that have been recognized through research as well as an agreement among specialists to be the best (at times called "prescribed procedures"). They will likewise assist you with indicating how you will decide if you are gaining ground.

What are the objectives and wanted results?

Objectives reflect what influences your desire to accomplish from here on out — they give the vision of the work you are doing and state what is to be achieved. Objectives are expansive articulations that frequently use various techniques related to accomplishing them. An objective ought to be founded on a portion of the requirements that you distinguished in Step 1.

Connected to an objective, an ideal result portrays how the objective populace could change given effective fulfillment of your techniques. Commonly, results are connected with changes in:

Information: What individuals realize or be aware of a subject (e.g., formative achievements for youngsters, the effect of smoking on a kid's wellbeing)
Mentalities: How individuals feel toward a theme (e.g., perspectives toward nurturing,

perspectives toward liquor and chronic drug use)

Abilities: The advancement of abilities (e.g., nurturing abilities, compromise strategies)

Ways of behaving: Changes in conduct (e.g., kid abuse, youngster conduct issues)

Wanted results make objectives more concrete, so that by changing these results, you draw nearer to the objective that you set.

How to foster objectives for your local area?

The objectives that you recognize ought to be legitimate by the needs that you distinguished because of your Step 1 work. An objective is an assertion of how you would like your local area to change because of the program that you carry out, so don't express your objective explanation as an action. "Carry out a home visiting program" is certainly not a valuable objective explanation; it doesn't depict how your work will work on the existence of youngsters and families. What's more, recollect — you needn't bother with plenty of objectives. A couple of good, clear objectives will assist you with remaining on track.

An ideal result is an explanation that makes objectives more concrete. To foster a valuable arrangement of wanted results (once in a while called targets or result in explanations), you should portray what explicit change(s) you desire to happen as an immediate consequence of your program that will assist you with accomplishing your objectives.

The CDC has fostered the idea of "Brilliant" results (Centers for Disease Control and Prevention, 2011). "Brilliant" can assist you with recollecting that an ideal result ought to be:

Explicit, depicting what will change (e.g., information, abilities, mentalities, ways of behaving), and for whom (e.g., moms, youngsters)
Quantifiable, zeroing in on how much change is normal
Reachable inside a given time
Sensible, precisely tending to the extent of the issue

Time-staged, showing when the result will be estimated.

You ought to have somewhere around one wanted result for every objective, and you can have multiple. The ideal results ought to be legitimately connected to help the accomplishment of the goal(s).

Business result

Wanted business results' are clear, explicit, and quantifiable meanings of the new end states you need to accomplish in the same old thing after the finish of the task when everything is working 'perfectly'.

The accomplishment of these results is what you need when you commission a task. They are your essential proportions of achievement.

The issue lies with what?

By far most ventures don't characterize the thing they are attempting to accomplish in a way that can be utilized to coordinate the undertaking and clarify what achievement is. They don't characterize clear, explicit, quantifiable business end states when "everything is working perfectly"- the ideal business results.

Rather they characterize targets, objectives, expectations, 'capacities', and different kinds of results, all of which come up short on accuracy and clearness required. Subsequently, the spotlight is a lot on the venture and what it is to do and convey, and insufficient on the business and what it needs to accomplish.

The ideal business results are frequently 'expected', lost in the consideration given to what the task needs to do — its arrangement, support, and conveyance. The undertaking administrator dominates and s/he is centered around what they need to do, convey and report. The business point of view, to the extent that it existed, gets derailed, neglected, and neither oversaw nor estimated.

Also, there is another convincing motivation behind why wanted business results are disregarded — individuals don't have the foggiest idea of how to characterize them.

However characterizing results is very straightforward and when you characterize the results you frequently decisively change the entire focal point of your task.

How can it function?
You want to begin with your targets, objectives, or explanations behind doing the undertaking — as you do today.
However at that point, taking each and every objective you inquire, "For what reason is that significant?"You rehash this inquiry utilizing the responses given posing "(Each response) Why is that significant?"

You proceed with this straightforward cycle until you run out of answers or you arrive at such a nonexclusive response that it is trivial (eg "To increment benefits").

Then, at that point, you examine your responses around the topics that have come from your responses and, for each subject, you compose a sentence that begins with, "We will find success when... " which gives you your most memorable draft result explanations.

That is all there is to it.

OK, there is a touch more refinement in the process than that, yet that is the cycle that changes 'projects' into 'business speculations'.

An illustration of how result articulations change the discussion

Allow me to give you a model.

Beginning goal: We need to move to new esteemed workplacesFor what reason is that significant? We need to be believed to be at the highest point of the market concerning quality and execution.

For what reason is that significant? We need to have the option to charge premium rates as befits the worth of our administrations

For what reason is that significant? We maintain that our administration quality should separate us.

For what reason is that significant? We are and should be viewed as a distinction firm that our clients need to be believed in to manage, After applying the TOP procedure to sort the subjects (Jigsaw Puzzle Sort) we get the genuine meaning of progress - a Desired Business Outcome proclamation, which characterizes:

"We will find true success when:

More than 90% of our exceptional paying clients keep on utilizing our administrations year on year since they recognize that they are getting profoundly esteemed administrations."
This draft result explanation is effectively quantifiable — Do over 90% of our superior paying clients stay with us every year or not? Indeed or no.

Presently the absolute first composition of this result explanation didn't contain the "more than 90%" or the "year-on-year" as these were added later to make the result more unambiguous and quantifiable with the goal that it very well may be a proportion of progress.

That is how it works — hence each draft result proclamation is exposed to audit and change until the assertion is 100 percent complete and addressed.

Notice the distinctions (and their effects)
Be that as it may, notice how the underlying goal was about us, "We need... " and the last assertion was about the client, "... our top notch paying clients... " In this model, the proposed office move is tied in with situating, marking, and maintenance of 'premium-paying clients'. There's no need to focus on working convenience.

Likewise, control of esteemed workplaces alone won't accomplish this result. The conveyed administrations should be of high worth and 'exceptionally esteemed' to legitimizc premium expenses. Consequently, substantially more than an office move is expected to accomplish this '90% maintenance' result — yet a significant number of these aspects would be missed on the off chance that the venture just centered around the workplace move undertakings.

The force of results
This is the force of result proclamations — they distinguish the genuine (business) justification

behind the venture and thus empower you to recognize ALL of the various sorts of exercises expected to accomplish these genuine business results.

In our model, those taking on this undertaking need to know who these clients are, what they esteem, where they are, and how they'll frequently come to the workplace, and that's just the beginning. The genuine business result and proportion of progress is superior client maintenance, not 'good' workplaces. The meaning of the ideal business results makes this understood.

Chapter 2

LESSEN THE LOSS OF AVERSION.

What is Loss Aversion?

Misfortune revolution is a mental inclination that portrays why, for people, the aggravation of losing is mentally two times as strong as the delight of acquiring. The misfortune felt from cash, or some other important article, can feel more regrettable than acquiring that equivalent thing.1 Loss revolution alludes to a singular's propensity to favor keeping away from misfortunes to getting identical increases. It's better not to lose $20, than to find $20.

We as a whole have the capacity to bear risk. A few of us need to develop boldness to take a stab at a novel, new thing, while others confront fears head-on, skydiving through life. The greatest gamble, notwithstanding, is keeping away from gambles out and out.

Pioneers can't remain safe and let the world cruise by, says Ram Charan, creator of The Attacker's Advantage: Turning Uncertainty Into

Breakthrough Opportunities. "At the right second, you really want the inward strength and conviction to take a jump when the result is dubious," he says.

Charan says daring people are impetuses, working in offense mode. "They're practitioners who face challenges dependent part of the way upon reality and part of the way on their creative mind about what could happen when those powers consolidate in what others could later call a union," he says. "The impetus, as a matter of fact, is the person who frequently makes the union."

Being OK with risk implies adjusting our outlook, says David Silverstein, creator of Three Steps Ahead and CEO of the procedure counseling firm BMGI. "Risk involves viewpoint; it's anything but a flat-out idea," he says. "At the point when I began my business, individuals thought I was a pioneering daring person. I, then again, felt like I was decreasing my own gamble by assuming command over my own predetermination as opposed to leaving myself in another person's hands."

Basic moves toward decreasing loss of Aversion

1. BEGIN WITH SMALL BETS
Believe the gamble to be a "try," which can feel more tasteful, says Roch Parayre, senior overseeing accomplice at the authority counseling firm Decision Strategies International and showing individuals at the Wharton School at the University of Pennsylvania.

"According to a gamble viewpoint, it permits pioneers to test development yet relieves risk in the event that circumstances don't work out as expected," he says.

2. ALLOW YOURSELF To ENVISION THE WORST-CASE SCENARIO
Silverstein calls this the indifferent way of thinking. "You can prepare yourself to take risks assuming you are really able to consider it and what can work out, and understand that the disadvantageous prospects aren't the apocalypse," he says. "Furthermore, the more

you have pondered something negative, the less startling it is the point at which it works out."

At the point when Silverstein's business went through a difficult stretch in 2009, for instance, he sat with his chief group and conceptualized what each would do in the event that the organization fizzled. "That gave them certainty that facing the challenge of remaining with the organization while we worked things through would be alright," he says.

3. FOSTER A PORTFOLIO OF OPTIONS
Assuming you've risked everything and the kitchen sink betting on just a single chance, you likely ought to stress over it, says Silverstein. All things considered, give yourself numerous opportunities for progress, and you're bound to be hopeful about the chance of something like one working out, he says.

Give yourself numerous opportunities for progress, and you're bound to be hopeful about the chance of something like one working out.
Parayre calls this the law of enormous numbers. "Seen in detachment, a singular drive might

appear to be excessively unsafe; assuming the drive bombs totally, you end up with nothing," he says. "In any case, in the event that you total each of the drives across an organization, or an individual's vocation, the law of enormous numbers will kick in and you can anticipate to a specific extent that they should succeed."

4. HAVE COURAGE TO NOT KNOW

Risk has a mental part, says Charan, and you really want a capacity to bear equivocalness.

"Going on the offense quite often requires making a move before you have a completely clear image of the relative multitude of variables your prosperity will rely upon," he says. "You should focus on another way ahead in any event, when a few things are fluffy, realizing that you will change your way en route."

5. TRY NOT TO CONFUSE TAKING A RISK WITH GAMBLING

Going on the offense doesn't give you consent to bet a business on hunches or hypotheses for which the potential outcomes are not thoroughly considered, says Charan. "Becoming mindful of and going up against your inward feelings of trepidation will permit you to see things all the more precisely, think all the more imaginatively, and move all the more conclusively," he says.

6. CLAIM YOUR EYES OFF OF THE REWARD
Embracing chance can likewise be scaring assuming you just spotlight on the result, says Margot Micallef, creator of It's the Landing That Counts. All things being equal, break risk into different little advances.
We can hardly stand to know everything-we won't ever will.
"Venturing out is frequently the most troublesome," she says. "The key is to keep on breaking the direction and the things to do down into increasingly small choices."

7. BE COMFORTABLE WITH GOOD ENOUGH
Something else that keeps individuals away from facing a challenge is the conviction that you can't begin until conditions are great, says Micallef.

"To embrace risk, we really want to dare to settle on choices with blemished data," she says. "We must be ready to course-right as more data opens up or as we hit road obstructions. Be that as it may, we can hardly hold on to know everything-we won't ever will."

Chapter 3

AGENDA THE IMPORTANCE OF YOUR DECISIONS.

Settling on choices can be unpleasant, baffling, and extreme. There are numerous interesting points prior to settling on a major choice. It appears to be in your twenties particularly that there are such countless gigantic choices to make: Deciding whether to move out of your family home, what to do after school, what you maintain that your profession should resemble, whether you need to get hitched, whether you need to have kids or a pet, whether you might want to travel, or on the other hand assuming that you ought to begin saving to possess a property or a new business.

At the point when you're in your late teenagers and mid twenties your greatest choices range from what breakfast you'll prepare the individual you connected with the previous evening to whether you truly need another jello shot. In view of this, it's conceivable that you might not have needed to handle any enormous choices and as a matter of fact you might suck at settling on choices overall.

This was absolutely me. Growing up I was a remarkably little accommodating person and I would never go with a choice because of a paranoid fear of culpable individuals, letting individuals down, or not having the option to say, "no" to individuals. As you grow up, fortunately your attitude changes in your twenties so I took in the most difficult way possible how to pursue extraordinary choices. So in the expectation of upgrading your dynamic cycle, the following are a lot of interesting points prior to going with significant groundbreaking choices.

1. Ask Yourself What You Really Want.
Does a corporate vocation seem like the most amazing job you could ever imagine or could you like to send off your own startup? Would you like to get hitched and have kids or would you like to invest a little energy soul looking and venturing to the far corners of the planet? There are so many streets you can take in your life, so it assists with understanding what you

truly need prior to settling on any enormous choices.

2. Request Advice.

Feel free to request guidance; it's anything but an indication of shortcoming, you're simply getting various perspectives on a circumstance and somebody might expose a point which you hadn't considered. Ask anybody — more seasoned family members, more youthful family members, companions, partners, outsiders — points should be considered to be as much as possible. Simply be careful about the well-known adage, "Such a large number of cooks ruin the stock." Don't allow others' viewpoints to pursue your choice completely for you.

3. Question Your Motives.

Is it safe to say that you are ascending the professional bureaucracy since you love your work or do you cherish the cash? Perhaps it's neither of these things and you're really doing it since it does right by your loved ones. Prior to taking the huge jump to stop a vocation which wasn't ideal for me, I asked myself, "Am I doing this for me or for others?" I before long acknowledged I was working a task I could have done without in light of the fact that it seemed like the reasonable choice and not on the grounds that it was satisfying me. The equivalent can be said for individuals near the very edge of other important choices: Are you getting hitched because you can't live without your accomplice or in light of the fact that every one of your companions are getting hitched? Could it be said that you are considering having a child since you can hardly stand to be a mother or on the grounds that you don't know how you need to manage your life yet? Posing yourself intense inquiries is truly hard however it assists with getting you to where you're intended to be.

4. Gauge The Pros and Cons.
There are advantages and disadvantages to all that throughout everyday life except weighing up the upsides and downsides of your potential decisions is an unquestionable necessity. You could do this with a companion, relative, or accomplice as they could have a totally alternate point of view to you. You can weigh up the

advantages and disadvantages of your future decisions by talking them through with somebody or in a real sense posting them on paper, on your PC, or telephone so you can see them clearly. Regardless of whether your favored decision has a greater number of cons than in addition to focus, your heart might in any case long for a specific bearing and it's certainly worth considering that. You might find a few sentiments which you didn't actually acknowledge you had!

5. Inquire as to whether You Will Be Hurting Yourself Or Others With Your Future Decision.
In spite of the fact that you may not understand it, each choice we make anyway affects others. You might be choosing whether to remain in a requesting position that gives you no free time for an immense raise. Indeed, the cash will be wonderful however you probably won't get time to appreciate it and you might experience the ill effects of business related pressure which could be awful for your wellbeing, which could likewise adversely influence the connections you have with your friends and family. Clearly in the event that you're choosing whether to

part ways with somebody or end a kinship for the right reasons, then, at that point, you are most likely going to put somebody in a bad mood in the short term, yet eventually, it will be the most ideal decision for both of you. Unnecessarily harming somebody with your decision is unique.

6. Check out At Your Potential Choices Without Rose Tinted Glasses

As of late, I was going to set out on a critical choice, however I was still stupidly wearing my rose colored exhibitions. I was examining some place I'd very much want to reside from now on; a delightful town in the English field where I would reside with my accomplice in a little house. Sounds pure, isn't that so? All things considered, in the wake of examining the choice with loved ones, I was made aware of the way that I had really been excessively hopeful about the entire thing. Obviously the town is really hard to enter and exit in the cold weather months, which would make it tricky for my accomplice to venture out to work. The exquisite cabins additionally profited from superb coal fires which really intended that there would be no focal warming, in this manner the cold weather months could get rather crisp. It's perfect to be hopeful, yet it's not OK to allow your positive thinking to daze you to the negatives of a possibly groundbreaking choice.

7. Envision What Your Dream Life Would Entail and See If Your Preferred Choice Fits Into It.

Subsequent to graduating, I am sorry to report that I abandoned my fantasy to be an essayist. I thought it appeared to be far-fetched that I would have the option to help myself by means of composing, thus I jumped starting with one work then onto the next that covered the bills, yet squashed my inventive soul. Ultimately I hit my limit. Throughout a couple of months, I had my quarter-life emergency and understood that I was most certainly not on the correct way and I had crushed my fantasies for a really long time. I went with a few truly terrifying choices which consolidated my fantasies and I am presently carrying on with a daily existence that I love. I feel truly glad for myself for taking seemingly a gigantic act of pure trust into the obscure, paying attention to my instinct, and placing confidence in my fantasies. Assuming you're in any way similar to me, you will stay unfulfilled until you can experience your fantasies. It pursues your choice making process and makes an easy decision in the event that your potential decision empowers you to carry on with your fantasy life.

Follow these tips and ideally your important choice will appear to be more similar to a mole slope than a mountain!

Chapter 4

BE SPEEDY IN SIMPLY DECIDING.

Regardless of whether you're choosing what to have for supper or whether to take on another undertaking, you're confronted with settling on many choices every day. Rather than feeling overpowered, permit yourself to pursue quick choices in view of the data you have. You'll presumably feel improved focusing on a decision and not re-thinking yourself. Additionally, the more frequently you go with fast choices, the better at it you'll get!

1. Utilize the 10-10-10 methodology for a significant choice.
Contemplate the future assuming you're pursuing a choice that has outcomes. Not certain on the off chance that you're content with your speedy choice? Give yourself a second to consider in the event that you'll be content with the result shortly, 10 months, and 10 years. In the event that you're settling on a low-outcome choice, such as purchasing a PC,

simply inquire as to whether you'll be blissful shortly and 10 months from now.

This is an extraordinary method for allowing yourself to break down without overthinking.

2. Pay attention to your gut feelings to settle on a natural choice.

Go with your stomach assuming you feel like one choice is superior to the others. You could observe that you're inclining toward one arrangement more than the others for not a great explanation other than you have an inclination. It's thoroughly alright to entrust yourself and run with that option!

For example, assuming you're attempting to conclude which course to sign up for, ask yourself, "Which one do I continue to return to?"

3. Utilize the course of end on the off chance that you have bunches of choices.

Consider every one of your decisions and recognize the one you're inclining toward. Then, contrast that choice and every one of your different decisions. Each time you intellectually think about, dispose of 1 decision so you'll be left with the most ideal choice. Go through them rapidly so you don't overthink conceivable outcomes.

For instance, in the event that you're attempting to rapidly settle on what to do throughout the end of the week, you could inquire as to whether you'd prefer to go setting up camp or see a film. Then, inquire as to whether you'd prefer to see a film or hit up a show. You'll manage your choices to concoct the most ideal decision.

4. Utilize the data you have for the quickest choice.

Analyze your current choices as opposed to social affairs more data. Assuming you begin exploring your choices, you could get overpowered or have an uncertain outlook on what to do. Additionally, you likely don't have a lot of time! All things considered, work with what you know and go from there.[4]

For example, in the event that you're attempting to rapidly pick a café to eat at, you could utilize the information on what's close by to go with a decision as opposed to getting on the web and perusing surveys for each eatery in the city.

In the event that it's really a speedy choice, you could have seconds or a couple of moments to pursue a decision. Any longer than this, and you'll likely make some harder memories focusing on a decision.

5. Depend on previous encounters to weigh results.

Recall whether you've settled on a comparable choice and in the event that you preferred the outcome. In the event that you needed to go with a speedy decision previously and it ended up good overall, you could pick a comparative choice. Notwithstanding, on the off chance that circumstances didn't pan out, consider doing things any other way this opportunity to get a superior outcome.

For example, on the off chance that companions inquire as to whether you might want to hang out at a bistro or do laser tag, you can promptly reference your involvement in laser tag to settle on a speedy choice.

6. Reevaluate the choice assuming that you esteem an external assessment.

Request that somebody present you with a suggestion. Assuming you're attempting to settle on a low-stakes choice that has a few outcomes however you're excessively occupied, ask a collaborator or your accomplice to concoct a proposal. This is particularly useful in the event that you're settling on a conclusion about something you don't have a clue about a great deal about.[6]
For example, on the off chance that you're looking for new tires and you have twelve choices that all appear to be something very similar to you, request that the agent give you 1 or 2 proposals. Once more, the stakes are low, so you simply have to go with a decision.

7. Focus on one decision so you don't overthink things.
It's not difficult to re-think yourself, however stay with your decision. Keep in mind, there's not a solitary "right" or "wrong" choice — and whenever you've settled on your fast choice,

there will continuously be something else to make!

You'll make it harder to pick in the event that you're apprehensive about the result. All things being equal, it could assist with contemplating what might occur assuming you sat idle. Much of the time, showing improvement over nothing so make sure to act!

8. Allow destiny to choose if you're totally uncertain.

Flip a coin or haphazardly pick on the off chance that your choice doesn't have outcomes. A ton of the minor choices we make are simply little subtlctics that don't actually influence us — what show would you like to watch? Which café would it be a good idea for you to eat at? Since there aren't any "off-base" replies, don't pressure with direction. Roll a kick the bucket, flip a coin, point your finger at a guide — the point is to pick something.

Chapter 5

BE SERIOUS LEANING.

Simple tasks on the most proficient method to be serious leaning..

1.STAYING CENTERED

1. Train your mind.
On the off chance that you experience difficulty remaining on track, it can assist with considering your cerebrum a muscle, and very much like your other muscles, it should be practiced to be compelling at its job.
Put away a period of day to work on zeroing in on a solitary undertaking.
Beginning little requires a couple of moments at first every day to truly make yourself completely center around a solitary errand. If and when you find your psyche meandering, quickly return to the main job.
Assuming you understand you've floated off task, that is around 50% of the fight!

2. Understand that all that you do has an outcome.

For each activity, there is an equivalent and inverse response. What you decide to do has results frequently in manners you can't anticipate or conceivably know about. Being serious includes perceiving what most requirements your consideration, and zeroing in on it.

Continuously stay away from hesitation. Besides the fact that hesitation causes pressure and adds to melancholy and nervousness, it tends to be a central point in diminishing by and large efficiency and prompting unseen side-effects.

Model: I want to manage a dead tree limb looming over my home. Rather I conclude I'll do it later and play a computer game at this point. Soon thereafter, my companion calls, and frantically needs a ride from the air terminal. The branch doesn't get managed. That evening there's a tremendous windstorm. The branch falls and pokes a hole in my rooftop. Presently, rather than just managing a tree limb, I nccd to sort my rooftop out, as well! Deal with what needs consideration first-you might think twice about it in the event that you don't.

3. Lessen the need to perform various tasks.
Performing various tasks causes us to feel like we're being useful, however as a general rule a lot performing various tasks can cause interruption and reduce our viability. Take each undertaking exclusively, make it happen, and continue on to the following.

4. Tackle your most troublesome assignments first.
Moving the most troublesome or least lovely undertakings first will give you an immense lift and decrease the chance of dawdling. Subsequent to moving the greatest hindrance, different things on your rundown will appear to be a breeze.

2. FOCUSING ON ERRANDS

1. Make a rundown.
Make a rundown the prior night of the day's errands arranged by direness and significance.

In the event that you have a cell phone, you have a strong hierarchical device readily available! There are numerous valuable applications for making a brief and supportive plan for the day. Utilizing an application can likewise assist you with keeping your rundowns coordinated, instead of making an ocean of paper.

Keep in mind, put the most troublesome undertakings at the first spot on your list.

2. Get up toward the beginning of the day and make your bed.

Beginning the day with a positive achievement, but little, gets the chunk of achievement until the end of the day rolling. Then, at that point, check your focus on rattle off. Take everything each in turn, and let each undertaking finish be a segue into the following. After each assignment is achieved, the following words out of a compelling and serious individual's mouth are, "what's straightaway?". Let that be your mantra. Continuously ask yourself, "what's straightaway?".

3. Permit yourself a brief break every now and then.

In any case, don't get derailed! Indicate what your break will involve. Think, "I'll complete this episode of my number one show while I eat this banana, then, at that point, return to the main job." Stick to it-once you let yourself slide off the timetable, it's a tricky slant to achieving nothing by any means.

4. Utilize your time shrewdly.

Perceive that time is limited, and consider it an asset. Know about the time you spend on an errand. Try not to turn out to be so cleared up in commonplace subtleties that you squander energy on things that don't make any difference. Ask yourself, "how can the time I'm spending on this propelling me toward my objective? Have the option to set things to the side that are keeping you away from achieving what you set off on a mission to achieve, or on the other hand, assuming that the manner in which you've decided to approach an undertaking isn't working, take a stab at something different. Be adaptable; be pliable. Have the option to twist without breaking.

5. Know how far you can go.

Realizing your cutoff points isn't restricting, yet liberating! Tolerating that you have achieved undertakings as well as could be expected is colossally fulfilling. Keep in mind, following through with any responsibility gives you a lift to achieve more. Make basic strides, and keep on doing as such, and over the long run you will achieve an extraordinary arrangement.

6. Grasp the standards of the game.

A few principles can be changed and others can't. Having the beauty to change what you can and acknowledge what you can't is immense in being a more serious individual. To worry about ordinary subtleties of life you wish could be unique, however realize where it counts can't, is to restrict yourself. At the point when you happen upon a steadfast snag, circumvent it, and continue on your course.

3. KEEPING A DEVELOPED AND PROFICIENT DISPOSITION

1. Look forward, not back.

As we become older, we will more often than not have any desire to hold tight to young ways of behaving. Everybody goes through times of contention between the craving to be lighthearted and simply have a good time, and being experienced and capable. We should confront it-frequently being adult and serious is the less promptly charming approach to carrying on with life. Nonetheless, being more serious in life includes understanding that the drawn out advantages of being dependable and getting it done offset gluttonous joys.

Wake regularly determined to be an adult.

Know every morning that a portion of the choices ahead in your day will include prior fun for achievement.

2. Think about your social height.

If you have any desire to be serious, know about how your ordinary way of behaving mirrors that. You are the way you act, so putting forth the attempt to be serious and mature in your activities over the course of the day, even the little things, is vital to genuinely being serious.

3. Be in charge of your feelings.

One of the main pieces of being experienced is being able to get a grip on your feelings, as opposed to them controlling you.

Consider your sentiments cautiously prior to following up on them. Act, don't respond. At the point when you act with development, you're utilizing the sane and thinking side of yourself as opposed to the carnal, instinctual side.

At the point when somebody addresses you, particularly in snapshots of contention, stop and consider your answer with a composed mind prior to answering. What initially jumps into your head isn't generally the best comment. Think before you talk.

Apply that to activities particularly. Talk is cheap, so be particularly mindful of how your activities ponder your degree of development. Do you act solely after coolly thinking out your course, or do you respond disregarding the results?

4. Love yourself.

Part of being experienced is perceiving that you have worth. It's frequently simpler to thump oneself over botches than to gain from them. [7] to be more experienced and carry on with a more serious life, put forth the attempt to regard yourself and worth yourself.

Approach your body with deference. Eat well, and get a lot of activity and rest.

Keep companions who esteem you, dispose of individuals who don't. Companions will regard you and comprehend that you are extraordinary for being you. Everybody encounters individuals who don't do those things. You have no commitment to keep them around. Some portion of development is settling on the extreme conclusions about who we partner with.

4. INVESTING HEAVILY IN YOURSELF AND YOUR APPEARANCE.

1. Be mindful (rather than reluctant).
Being mindful doesn't mean you are being bashful or humiliated, viewpoints we typically partner with reluctance, however that you have the ability to think about yourself, both deep down and obviously.

2. Practice great cleanliness.

Investing heavily in oneself enough to rehearse great cleanliness is significant in being a serious and significant individual. It is additionally better and will just assist you with feeling far better!

Keep your hair and fingernails managed.

Clean your teeth something like two times a day. Rehearsing great oral cleanliness not just shows others that you are a significant and assembled individual, however it likewise safeguards against bacterial disease and is gainful for your wellbeing in general.

3. Wear garments that you like, flawlessly.

Wearing garments that you need to wear, and that are flawless, is significant in showing that you are a significant individual. It doesn't need to imply that you are vain or excessively unsure, yet basically that you care sufficiently about your own prosperity to deal with yourself.

5. RECALLING THE BRILLIANT RULE.

1. Be useful to other people.

It is so natural in this day and age to become zeroed in on "me" that we frequently fail to remember that perhaps the most fulfilling and useful thing we can do is to zero in on the prosperity of others.

At the point when you are useful to other people, even in little, ordinary ways, you will observe that your general feeling of your own prosperity will enormously increase and your trust in the errands and objectives you have before you will be a lot more prominent.

More prominent trust in yourself and your own capacities brings about a lot higher individual efficiency, and, thus, will assist you with turning into a more serious individual.

2. Volunteer.

Engage in nearby workers' valuable open doors. In 2013 alone, north of 62 million Americans took part in some type of humanitarian effort.

Do you have a weakness for youngsters? For old timers? For creatures? Perhaps you might want to assist with keeping up with trails at a nearby park, or feed the destitute in a soup kitchen. Volunteer open doors flourish all over the place, particularly in metropolitan habitats.

Indeed, two or three hours every week, or even a month, can assist with providing you with a feeling of concentration and motivation in your life. Chipping in not just helps you have a positive outlook on yourself, it associates you with others, expands your interactive abilities, battles wretchedness, and helps keep you healthy.[10]

3. Practice the brilliant rule.
At the point when you do to others as you would have done to yourself, you make a circle of generosity. This isn't only for the well-being of ethical quality; the more you show generosity to other people, the more certain they will be to add to your own progression.

Tips
Make an opportunity to stride back and see what you've accomplished. Keep in mind, having a deep satisfaction about achieving will assist with rousing you to achieve significantly more. You live in a climate, so make it amazing. Encircle yourself with you. Set aside some margin to clean, to outfit your home and work area and make it your own. At the point when

you are in charge of your current circumstance,
you are in charge of yourself.

Chapter 6

MAKE A RUNDOWN OF THE SIGNIFICANT DO'S TO KEEP AWAY FROM.

Basic instrument to coordinate everything
It's a rundown of errands you want to finish or things that you need to do.
Do any of the accompanying appear to be natural?
 Frequently feel totally wrecked with how much work you must do?
You now and again neglect to do things that are significant
Individuals need to pursue you to finish things
You track down it a battle to keep to cut off times
Try not to believe you're uncommon in light of the fact that there are a huge number of individuals who battle with a similar situation consistently, in the work environment as well as in their own life as well. Fortunately, there is something extremely straightforward you can do to keep your life and work more coordinated. Get everything rolling, Request a Welcome

What is a Lineup for the day?
The definition is a basic one. It's a rundown of undertakings you really want to finish or things that you need to do.
Most ordinarily, they're coordinated and arranged by need. Generally, they're composed on a piece of paper or post notes and go about as a memory help. As innovation has developed we have had the option to make schedules with success bookkeeping sheets, word reports, email records, lineup for the day applications, Microsoft to do and research plan for the day to give some examples. You can involve a plan for the day in your home and individual life, or in the work environment.
Having a rundown of all that you want to do recorded in one spot implies you shouldn't fail to remember anything significant. By focusing on the undertakings in the rundown you plan the request in which you will do them and can rapidly see what needs your quick consideration and what errands you can leave until somewhat later.

The Advantages of Utilizing a Plan for the day.

Quite possibly the main explanation you ought to utilize a plan for the day is that it will assist you with remaining coordinated. At the point when you compose every one of your errands in a rundown, they appear to be more reasonable. At the point when you have an unmistakable diagram of the errands you must do and those you've finished, it assists you with remaining on track. While opening up space to you for other more inventive assignments.

At the point when you complete an undertaking, you can check it off your rundown. This provides you with a feeling of progress and accomplishment, something you'll need on the off chance that you're continuously surging starting with one errand then onto the next. In the event that you feel a pride, it spikes you on and persuades you to continue to push ahead.

Yet, that is not by any means the only advantage of a plan for the day. The following are a couple of something else:

Works on your memory:
A plan for the day goes about as an outside memory help. Holding a couple of snippets of

data all at once is just conceivable. Keep a plan for the day and you'll have the option to monitor everything, instead of only a couple of the errands you really want to do. Your plan for the day will likewise build up the data, which makes it doubtful you will fail to remember something.

Increments efficiency:
A plan for the day permits you to focus on the undertakings that are more significant. This implies you don't throw away life on errands that don't need your quick consideration. Your rundown will assist you with remaining fixed on the undertakings that are the most significant.

Assists with inspiration:
Plans for the day are an extraordinary persuasive instrument since you can utilize them to explain your objectives. You can partition your drawn out objective into more modest, more attainable momentary objectives and as you tick every oddball your rundown, your certainty will increase.

What is a Schedule in business and for what reason is it significant?

It appears to be a particularly basic arrangement by investing pen to paper and removing energy from your day to make a plan for the day, an arrangement for your day characterizes your difficulties and objectives. Keeping time from being squandered attempting to distinguish what is the following most significant undertaking to handle straight away and, surprisingly, more significant ensures you remember to accomplish something significant.

Plans for the day offer a method for expanding efficiency, preventing you from failing to remember things, focus on errands, oversee undertakings successfully, use time carefully and further develop using time effectively as well as the work process.

What Makes an Extraordinary Plan for the Day Application?

Daily agendas come in all shapes and sizes. It generally used to be something that you would compose utilizing pen and paper, yet on account of innovation there's an application that can act the hero. What compels a decent plan for the day application?

Errands ought to be quick to add and arrange

There ought to be various ways of sorting out the undertakings

Capacity to design your work process

Laying out boundaries

Updates for any deliberate cutoff times.

Designation of undertakings if involving it for tasks of the executives with a group. Group plan for the day permits you to appoint the most qualified individual.

Ready to synchronize between various stages

Everything necessary is only a couple of moments consistently to keep a plan for the day exceptional. With a plan for the day, you can finish objectives without having nothing to do attempting to sort out needs. Your efficiency will increase, you will not fail to remember things, your time usage can improve and you'll deal with your undertakings all the more really.

Chapter 7

MAKE AN AGENDA OF INDIVIDUAL CHOICE AND IMPROVEMENT.

Individual choices help in our day to day exercises and vocations..
The following are a couple of demonstrated strides on the most proficient method to fabricate our own choices and improvement...

1. CONCEPTUALIZING YOUR ERRANDS

1. Conclude what medium turns out best for you.

On the off chance that your cell phone is in your grasp the entire day consistently, utilize the Notes application to make your daily agenda. In the event that you disdain gazing at a telephone or PC screen, snatch a pen or pencil and compose your rundown the hard way. A plan for the day won't be useful in the event that you fear making it or utilizing it, so pick anything medium you favor most.

2. List every one of the errands that you want to achieve.

These can go from "Shower" to "Finish show for work one week from now" to "Track down a present for Mother's birthday one month from now." As may be obvious, these undertakings range in their tendency, their significance, and the time they will take. Try not to stress over following an example of coordinating them — that will happen later. For the time being, simply record each liability you consider.

Composing without question, everything down, you will forget about it and onto paper. It will guarantee you remember anything, and ideally, it will likewise assist your brain with feeling less packed.

The running rundown of each and every errand you have on your radar will be alluded to as your lord list.

3. Re-appropriate any assignments you can.

After you've recorded the things you want to do, choose if you can enroll any assistance. This is particularly significant assuming you are overpowered or crunched for time. Don't hesitate for even a moment to request help, delegate obligations, and fight the temptation to obsessively hover over. On the off chance that it needn't bother with being on your to-do radar, eliminate it.

2. ARRANGING YOUR ERRANDS.

1. Sort your lord list into classifications.
For instance, you might have a plan for the day for work and a plan for the day for home. By making separate records, you can concentrate and energy on each arrangement of undertakings in turn. It is a waste of time to take a gander at your own plan for the day while you're sitting in your office, so set it aside!
To be generally useful, you really want to have limited focus on the undertakings before you. Eliminate the foundation commotion and the pressure of future errands by making circumstance explicit records.

2. Make your plans for the day for the ongoing day as it were.
 Keep it basic! This will assist you with putting together your errands arranged by need, and

you won't feel overpowered looking forward to assignments for later, one week from now, or one month from now. Be reasonable about what you can achieve in 24 hours. Your everyday daily agendas ought to have under ten things, and perhaps under five.

In the event that you can't sort out where to begin, attempt this. Envision you quick forward to sleep time. Which undertaking would you like to be done with first? That ought to be at the first spot on your list.

Utilize your lord rundown to make your day to day records. After you've made your day to day list, set your lord list aside.

3. Gauge the time each errand will take.

Be practical! Assuming that you over-commit yourself and continually feel like you're using up all available time to finish your rundown, you will make pointless pressure. It's difficult to be useful assuming that you're feeling bothered. Close to each undertaking, write down what amount of time you really think everyone will require. Utilize these time evaluations to design your day.

Provide yourself with a pad of 10 to 15 minutes between each undertaking. Sensibly you can't change starting with one task then onto the next with next to no progress time, so consider this while you're making your timetable.

4. Make your rundown tastefully satisfying.
This might sound shallow or superfluous, however it truly can assist with significantly altering the manner in which you take a gander at your plan for the day. Compose or type it out in your #1 variety. Compose on a piece of writing material, post it on a beautiful notice board, or make a smooth record on your cell phone. Simply make a rundown that moves you to remain propelled and have things looked at off.

3. CONSIDERING YOURSELF RESPONSIBLE

1. Record due dates close to each undertaking on your lord list.
These will help you as you are making your day to day plans for the day. At the point when you have countless assignments, it is not difficult to allow things coincidentally to escape everyone's

notice. As you make your everyday rundown every day, go over your lord rundown and ensure you incorporate any errand with impending due dates.

In the event that there is no due date for a specific undertaking, settle on a practical date you'd truly prefer to have it done by.

In the event that you're not defining objectives for yourself, the less critical things might in all likelihood never finish.

2. Put your plan for the day somewhere you will see it routinely.

It is an exercise in futility to make a rundown on the off chance that you push it in a cabinet and just drop it. Ensure you are continually seeing it! You might feel that you will not fail to remember anything or that you'll remain useful, however genuinely seeing a rundown of errands you really want to achieve can truly get the inspirational fire going inside you.

Heft it around with you. Post it in your restroom. Leave a duplicate in your tote and your vehicle. Just put it somewhere where it will be right in front of you.

3. Share your rundown with somebody.
It tends to be a parent, a companion, a critical other, or a collaborator. Simply ensure somebody will determine the status of your rundown and ask about your advancement. You likely won't feel far better in the event that you tell somebody you scratched nothing off your plan for the day for an entire day!
You needn't bother with a sitter, and nobody most likely needs to be your sitter. In any case, it is unimaginably useful to have somebody considering you responsible.

Chapter 8

CHALLENGE YOUR ASSUMPTIONS

You might have heard that familiar saying in regards to what befalls you and me when you expect. That maxim has failed to understand the situation. To be compelling as an item individual, you need to make presumptions to begin work on an item. What truly creates some issues is the point at which you don't challenge those suppositions. All things considered, there are great and terrible ways of testing suspicions. Here are a few assets that will assist you with testing suppositions in a useful manner without making you fall off like a jackass.

Suspicions are much of the time an unavoidable piece of speedy direction, yet tolerating suppositions as reality can be unsafe to your business and workers.

I realized this the most difficult way possible quite a while back when I was essential for an exhibition on board stage execution at LandAmerica Financial Group. The stage was "cutting edge," and we were eager to approach information about execution, and surrendered that until that point, we had no quantifiable method for estimating it. Yet, halfway through execution we understood that the greater part of the leaders who might need to utilize the program missed the mark on PC abilities expected for the new innovation.

For this situation, we had expected everybody had a similar degree of IT experience as the HR division — and didn't ponder other possible clients. Our presumptions prompted a quick at the end of the day terrible choice that harmed our interior standing and disappointed clients. To keep this from occurring from now on, I thought of a speedy agenda to guarantee we wouldn't misstep the same way once more.

Follow these three stages and abandon your suspicions for a more essential dynamic interaction — one that will be especially valuable for executing new programming.

1) ORGANIZE THE DECISION MAKING

One method for becoming more vital about navigation is to utilize authoritative apparatuses that guide the reasoning system.

These apparatuses help sort, orchestrate and examine significant information. Furthermore, there are hundreds accessible, going from straightforward conceptualizing advances to complex ones. Devices that mechanize the PDCA (Plan, Do, Check, Act) way to deal with direction, for instance, help lay out a restrained, agenda driven process for making moves.

Process-situated programming can assist with smoothing out extreme hierarchical issues, for example, carrying out another innovation. A decent dynamic device will assist you with distinguishing every key partner, include them all the while and offer them the chance to show up, which will settle on choice making more careful and truth based, as opposed to suspicion based.

2) ASK YOURSELF TOUGH QUESTIONS

Proactively expecting the difficulties that will emerge because of any choice you make can go quite far in forestalling likely traps. The following are three fundamental inquiries that you ought to constantly pose prior to pursuing choices that include others.

Does the organization have satisfactory assets? Most executions require equal cycles — making all the difference for the old interaction, while testing another one. However, assuming that the representatives entrusted with keeping up with both the new and the old are as of now over-burden, they won't be valid analyzers. To decide whether you have the right assets, you want observational information including the volume of work being added, the volume of work being gotten rid of, and the data transmission of existing staff.

Do laborers have the expected abilities and information? An aggregate conversation that contrasts the ongoing system and the new cycle can raise information necessities that you may not be thinking about.

Is this the ideal opportunity? In the event that your assets will be deficient, or on the other hand assuming you decide there is re-skilling fundamentals, you should challenge your timetable. Assuming the timing is projected in concrete, essentially you'll know about potential leaks going in, and can address them.

3. APPROACH COLLEAGUES TO SPEAKUP

Provoking partners to voice their interests about impending choices and changes offers a profundity of survey. This is basic in light of the fact that the more info you accumulate previously, during and after another execution, the more proprietorship individuals will feel for the final result. Furthermore, a more prominent feeling of pride implies laborers are bound to jump aboard with a choice that has been made, and take the necessary steps to make it work.

Neglecting to request input from the whole group that will be affected by a choice over and over again brings about hiccups during execution —, for example, individuals not having what it takes expected to utilize the innovation — which thus can prompt absence of reception.

Bringing all partners into a choice and listening cautiously to their feedback can assist lead with bettering dynamics in general. One illustration that has remained with me all through my vocation is that there are covered landmines of suspicion in each choice, and the more individuals that gander at their choices, the more noteworthy their possibility of finding these landmines before its past the point of no return.

Photograph: Creative Commons

Plan a customized 1:1

Converse with a Cornerstone master about how we can assist with your association's remarkable individuals the executives need.

Chapter 9

DISREGARD THE SUNK COST FALLACY.

What is a Sunk Cost?

A sunk expense is an expense that has previously happened and can't be recuperated using any and all means. Sunk costs are autonomous of any occasion and ought not be thought about while going with venture or task choices. Just pertinent expenses (costs that connect with a particular choice and will change contingent upon that choice) ought to be thought about while pursuing such choices.

All sunk expenses are viewed as fixed costs. Nonetheless, it is essential to understand that not all decent expenses are viewed as sunk costs. Review that sunk expenses can't be recuperated. Take, for instance, hardware (a proper expense). Hardware can be exchanged or returned at a decided cost. In this manner, it's anything but a sunk expense.

Sunk cost is otherwise called past expense, inserted cost, earlier year cost, abandoned cost, sunk capital, or review cost.

Instances of Sunk Costs

Assume you purchase a pass to a show for $150. The evening of the show, you recall that you have a significant task due on that very night. You should settle on a choice: hit up the show or finish your task. The $150 paid for the ticket is a sunk expense and shouldn't influence your choice.

An organization burns through $5 million on building a plane. Preceding finish, the supervisors understand that there is no interest in the plane. The flight business has developed and carriers request an alternate sort of plane. The organization has a decision: finish the plane for another $1 million or fabricate the new popular plane for $4 million. In this situation, the $5 million previously spent on the old plane is a sunk expense. It shouldn't influence the choice and the main important expense is the $4 million.

An organization burns through $10,000 preparing its workers to utilize another ERP framework. The product ends up being intensely confounding and questionable. The senior supervisory group needs to cease the utilization of the new ERP framework. The $10,000 spent to prepare representatives is a sunk expense and ought not be viewed as in that frame of mind of stopping the new ERP framework.

An organization burns through $10 million to lead a showcasing study to decide the benefit of another item they will send off in the commercial center. The review reasons that the item will be vigorously fruitless and unrewarding. In this way, the $10 million is a sunk expense. The organization shouldn't go on with the item send off and the underlying advertising concentrate on venture ought not be thought about while simply deciding.

The Sunk Cost Fallacy

The sunk expense deception thinking states that further speculations or responsibilities are legitimate on the grounds that the assets previously contributed will be lost in any case. Thus, the sunk expense false notion is a slip-up in thinking wherein the sunk expenses of a movement are thought about while choosing whether to go on with the action. This is additionally frequently known as "wasting valuable resources."

Expect you to burn through $200 on a snowboarding trip at Grouse Mountain. Later on, you find a superior snowboard trip at Cypress Mountain that costs $100 and you buy that ticket too. Unconsciously, you figure out that the two dates conflict and you can't have the money in question returned on the tickets. Could you go to the $200 great snowboard trip or the $100 extraordinary snowboard trip?

A larger part of individuals would pick the more costly outing on the grounds that, despite the fact that it may not be more enjoyable, the misfortune appears to be more noteworthy. The sunk expense paradox keeps you from acknowledging what the most ideal decision is and makes you put more noteworthy emphasis on the deficiency of unrecoverable cash.

Instances of the Sunk Cost Fallacy

In the accompanying models, you can plainly perceive what sunk costs mean for direction.

Sunk costs make individuals think unreasonably.

Tom buys a film ticket online for $12.50 and after showing up at the performance centers to watch the film, Tom understands that the film is truly exhausting and doesn't engage him. Tom chooses to endure the whole film since he previously purchased a ticket.

Jennifer pays a $100 section charge to join a new mentoring club. In the wake of going to 4 of the 7 meetings, Jennifer concludes that the coaching meetings facilitated by the club don't help her by any means. She chooses to go to the leftover 3 meetings in spite of it being pointless due to the $100 section expense.

Applications in Financial Modeling

It's significantly simpler to keep away from the sunk expense error in monetary demonstrating, as DCF models just gander at future incomes, and give no thought to the past.

Hence, it very well may be useful for a monetary expert to play out the activity of building a monetary model in Excel to eliminate any inclination (connected with sunk expenses) and take a gander at anything that boosts the Net Present Value going ahead.

Outline

In both financial matters and business direction, sunk cost alludes to costs that have previously occurred and can't be recuperated. Sunk costs are prohibited from future choices in light of the fact that the expense will be the equivalent no matter what the result.

The sunk expense deception emerges while dynamic considers sunk costs. By thinking about sunk costs while pursuing a choice, unreasonable navigation is shown.

Chapter 10

KEEP AWAY FROM INFORMATION OVERLOAD

What Is Information Overload?
Data over-burden is the tricky course of attempting to comprehend something and settle on the ideal choice when we have an excessive amount of data about the thing we're attempting to choose. The term comes from a book, The Managing of Organizations, composed by friendly researcher Bertram Gross and distributed in 1964. However, it almost certainly turned out to be important for the public vernacular with the distribution of the top rated Future Shock by Alvin and Heidi Toffler in 1970.

The Tofflers characterized data over-burden as happening "when how much contribution to a framework surpasses its handling limit. Chiefs have genuinely restricted mental handling limits. Therefore, when data over-burden happens, all things considered, a decrease in choice quality will happen."

We should place it in additional brilliant terms: recollect those old science fiction motion pictures where an individual beats the oppression of some underhandedly tyrant PC by suggesting an irrational conversation starter? Smoke surges from its worn out hardware as it battles to work out the endless. We aren't PCs, however we can blow our own variant of gaskets when we're over-burden with an excess of information. It gums up the hardware and our minds slow down as our eyes roll back in our minds, defeat by decision.

Risks of Information Overload
Regardless of whether it has a name, data over-burden has been around insofar as individuals have assembled data. It spikes with progress in innovation, for example, in the Renaissance when compositions were saved by replicating old texts. Be that as it may, it stems considerably further back to the Bible, where it's alluded to in the book of Ecclesiastes 12:12, where it's said, "Of making books there is no closure."

A survey by the Pew Research Center noticed that 20% feel over-burden with data, which makes pressure, particularly on the off chance that a task has high data requests for its workers. In any case, not just pressure at work shows; data over-burden can be analyzed through numerous side effects.

1. Cerebrum Fog
You've heard the maxim "mind haze"? A mind is an astonishing device, one that we've just tapped as far as its true capacity, yet even it has its cutoff points. We frequently surpass what our minds can process and in this manner arrive at something many refer to as mental over-burden, and that implies we hit a psychological wall that prompts peevishness and unfortunate reasoning.

This innately will lessen one's capacity to use sound judgment, making us more inclined to consistent false notions. Our psyches get drained and pursuing a choice takes energy, which is depleted during the time spent social occasion information. This affects your direction, yet your efficiency and capacity to remain inspired too. Does that cause you to feel restless? Indeed, that is one more side effect of data over-burden.

Instructions to Avoid Information Overload.
We live in a data immersed age and on occasion it could feel difficult to keep away from. Most don't have the privilege to go off the lattice or join a cloister. However, that doesn't mean one ought to surrender, surrender and hop in the unending stream of information to suffocate in pieces and bytes.
The Buddhists discuss a central way, which is simply control. It's a clear headed method for moving toward data, where balance implies limitation instead of restraint. The possibility that one can keep away from data is absurd and not viable. In any case, there are ways not to indulge. Here are only seven — we would rather not overpower you.

1. Turn off.
The majority of us go through our work time on earth online to some limit or summary of enormous areas of information. Then we get back home and suck up more data, falling into a

dark opening of the web or virtual entertainment.

Help your cerebrum out and get off the PC for a couple of hours consistently, and try to debilitate those irritating warnings. Simply find an opportunity to sit idle. Be languid. Indeed, even stay away from papers or books. There are care rehearsals in the event that you really want some direction, however sitting and being non judgemental present with your viewpoints and sentiments surprisingly go can be exceptionally remedial. It allows your psyche an opportunity to reboot and charge its psychological batteries.

2. Deal with Your Information.

Turning off probably won't be a choice working, so you must adopt another strategy. There's an assault of data at work yet that doesn't mean you need to answer it promptly when it lands in your inbox.

Be more specific and focus on your data. At the point when you receive an email, undoubtedly you can tell from the headline whether it needs a fast reaction or on the other hand on the off chance that you can set it to the side for some time. Then have a devoted period during the day wherein you can go through your correspondences. Remember a spam channel to hold the volume to a sensible flood. These are key methods and instruments for emailing the executives.

3. Get Everyone Involved.
There's just so much you can do on your own in an office. While essential to control the data crosses your work area, there is additionally more aggregate information that is past your power. You should foster a brought together front, and send functional greatness, to overcome this intruder.

That implies formulating a data procedure at work. Get purchase from associates, who ought to be available for any reason to diminish the trading of pointless data. That could mean downplaying desk work and just when fundamental and keeping gatherings right on track by having a characterized and explicit plan. Obviously, updating your venture the board programming can assist with decreasing superfluous strides too.

4. Keep It Simple.
Data is excess in the event that it's copied. You needn't bother with a duplicate of everything, and you positively don't have any desire to get a similar notification again and again. In this way, put forth a valiant effort to ensure individuals know how to contact you, so they don't immerse each channel that can set you up to ensure you get their note.

That implies, be expressive about whether you lean toward email, text or another type of correspondence. Assuming that they need affirmation, let them tell you so you can answer, instead of having them call you to ensure you've accepted their message. Momentous how much data an individual gets simply says exactly the same thing on an alternate stage. (In the event that you're running an undertaking, this is where a venture correspondence plan can assist with explaining how the data will be dispersed.)

5. Clear Your Mind
Consider it housework. On the off chance that you don't clear occasionally, you'll have a

zoological display of residue rabbits. On the off chance that you don't clear your head, the significant data will make some harder memories getting the obstacles free from all that psychological garbage. Consequently, a normal "mind dump" is an extraordinary method for resetting your head and keeping that bothersome data over-burden under control.

One method for doing this is as it was done in the good 'ol days, with pen and paper. Record each belief that is interfering with your work. It's odd, yet when they're on paper, they're somewhere far away from me. As it were, it permits your mind to zero in on different things since you've put away data that was obstructing it on a paper, the first outside hard drive.

6. Put down certain boundaries.
There's something many refer to as the two-minute rule, and that implies spending just two minutes on an undertaking. This is basically giving yourself limits. One issue with data is that today there is in every case more and it's effectively available. From regarded

sources to recounted references, master guidance and critique to conclusions and tirades, there's no limit to any subject.

In any case, you can stop that with this time usage system. Give yourself limits, which references are significant, and which are not? Likewise, how long merits the inquiry and when does that time turn into an obstruction to pursuing a choice? Center around the subject in question, don't perform various tasks, yet give the inquiry the time it merits and afterward pull the trigger on the choice.

7. Get ready for the Next Day.
Indeed, you traversed one day without data over-burden, presently it is the ideal time to set up the close to be as fruitful. This ought to be a day to day practice, best to do it before you go home in the event that you're contemplating the workplace, or before you hit the sack on the off chance that the objective is more private. This center is a focused method for monitoring data over-burden.

One method for doing this is by posting the main few assignments you need to handle the following day. Focus on them in a rundown to gather your contemplations about the approaching day, which will likewise help you not sit around idly or energy on overthinking the work or being not able to oversee it since it's quickly becoming due and breathing down your neck.

Was that a lot of data to take ready? Ideally, it'll demonstrate accommodations and make your head clear to deal with the day's worth of effort. Whenever you have the right outlook, then, at that point, now is the ideal time to outfit yourself with the right apparatuses. ProjectManager is a cloud-based project of the executives programming that works with a work process with kanban sheets, task records and a cooperative stage. Deal with your data better with ProjectManager by requiring this free 30-day preliminary today.

Chapter 11

MENTAL MODELS HELPS IN MAKING BETTER DECISIONS.

What are mental models?

Mental models are systems that provide individuals with a portrayal of how the world functions. There are so many mental models that it would require an extremely lengthy investment to concentrate on them all exhaustively. Some are established in natural perceptions, others have been depicted in conduct studies.

To lay it out plainly, mental models are a bunch of convictions and thoughts that we intentionally or unknowingly structure in light of our encounters. They guide our considerations and ways of behaving and assist us with grasping life. They're essentially thinking apparatuses — alternate ways for thinking.

For example, realizing about network impacts or about the pattern of consistent, unavoidable losses assists you with contemplating frameworks. Being familiar with motivating forces or the accessibility heuristic assists you with contemplating human connections. Being familiar with exchange and shortage assists you with pondering business sectors and financial patterns.

I have forever been captivated by mental models. The same way researchers are searching for a hypothesis of everything, I once in a while keep thinking about whether there is a widespread hypothesis of the psyche. A sweeping, intelligible structure that would completely make sense of and connect together all parts of our science and brain research.
While mental models are essential to comprehend how our psyche functions, they're quite flawed. They should be utilized in setting, and frequently in blend. As numerous psychological models are intelligent of the intricacies of human instinct, some are likewise great to be aware of to try not to succumb to them.
Think better with these 10 models
Here is a rundown of key mental models that you can begin examining and seeing in your day

to day routine at the present time, in sequential request. I might add more from here on out, however 30 is a lot to begin.

1. Securing:

A mental predisposition where a singular depends too vigorously on an underlying snippet of data — the "anchor" — while deciding.

 2. In reverse affixing:

Working in reverse from your objective.

3. Old style molding:

You've most likely caught wind of Pavlov's canine. Traditional molding is a learning technique wherein an organically intense boost — like food — is matched with a formerly nonpartisan upgrade — suppose a ringer. The unbiased boost comes to make a reaction (salivation) that is normally like the one made by the strong upgrade (for this situation, food).

4. Responsibility and consistency predisposition:

The longing to be and seem reliable with what we have proactively done.

5. Common sense:

information that is known by everybody or almost everybody, typically regarding a specific local area. Common sense isn't guaranteed to mean truth, however the vast majority will acknowledge it as legitimate.

6. Similar benefit:

The capacity to complete a specific monetary movement — like making a particular item — more proficient than another action.

7. Broadening:

The most common way of dispensing your assets in a manner that lessens the openness to any one specific gamble.

8. Economies of scale:

The expense benefits that organizations acquire because of their size of activity. The bigger the scale, the more modest the expense per unit.

9. Productive market speculation:

A hypothesis that expresses that costs completely mirror all suitable data. The speculation suggests that it ought to be difficult to reliably beat the market, since market costs ought to just respond to new data.

10. Game hypothesis:

An umbrella term for the study of sensible dynamics in people, creatures, and PCs.

The most effective method to utilize mental models

On the off chance that the sum total of what you have is a sledge, all that seems to be a nail. A typical misinterpretation is that psychological models ought to be obediently polished and applied to work on your psychological execution. There are really numerous psychological models which you ought to endeavor to stay away from. For instance, having an "deception of control" can be especially perilous in certain circumstances.

Mental models:

Conduct, result, support

To develop as an individual, you should have the option to recognize mental models, whether you are utilizing them, or the individual you are conversing with is. Preferably, you want to pursue a cognizant decision to utilize them or not, rather than succumbing to the programmed thinking our cerebrum cherishes so beyond a doubt.

"To break a psychological model is more diligently than parting the iota."

Albert Einstein (however likely not)

So how might you challenge your psychological models, distinguish them in others, and use them in a way that is really successful and valuable?

The following are a couple of tips you can apply to dominate mental models, as opposed to being oppressed by them.

Know about your reasoning by asking yourself inciting inquiries

Accumulate data to challenge your reasoning with undeniable realities

Ask into others' reasoning and challenge their perspectives

Oppose rushing to make judgment calls and suspend your suspicions

Search for repeating thought designs and forget them

A device is just on par with what its client. Just once you're mindful of your psychological models, you can utilize them actually to accomplish your objectives.

The most effective method to fabricate your own psychological models

In a quick climate, mental models can be very valuable to help you think quickly and decide. All things considered, they're perfect at giving you basic guidelines so you can, whenever gotten along nicely, foresee likely results or ways of behaving.

1. Notice individuals.

One extraordinary method for fostering your own psychological models is to track down motivation in individuals. When you read a memoir, ask yourself: for what reason did they settle on this choice? What were they thinking? What mental model(s) did they utilize? It doesn't need to be well known business people or creatives. We as a whole have a companion or a partner whose work we respect. At the point when you see them go with a particular decision in a complicated circumstance, ask them how they came to that choice.

2. Observe nature.

Nature adheres to numerous guidelines that can apply to human navigation. For instance, the propensity to limit our energy result can be seen in numerous regular circumstances, and motivations are a key drive in the entirety of animals' way of behaving.

3. Request criticism.
Ask a companion or a partner to see how you act and to assist you with distinguishing ways of behaving that may not be clear to you. This can be an unimaginably awkward yet mind-growing activity.
Try not to restrict yourself to valuable mental models. You will notice mental models which you'd prefer not to imitate. These are perfect to concentrate too, on the grounds that it's simpler to keep away from an idea design when you know how to detect it in yourself as well as other people. Useful or damaging, name your psychological models and get them on paper.

Chapter 12

PICK FROM A LIMITED OPTIONS.

Choices can be utilized to carry out a wide cluster of exchanging techniques, going from basic trade to complex spreads with names like butterflies and condors. What's more, choices are accessible on an immense scope of stocks,currencies,commodities, trade exchanged assets, and prospects contracts.

There are many strike costs and lapse dates accessible for every resource, which can represent a test to the choice fledgling in light of the fact that the plenty of decisions accessible makes it once in a while hard to distinguish a reasonable choice to exchange.

KEY TAKEAWAYS
Choices exchanging can be intricate, particularly since a few unique choices can exist on the equivalent hidden, with various strikes and lapse dates to look over.

Tracking down the best choice to accommodate your exchanging procedure is thus fundamental to boost progress on the lookout.

There are six essential moves toward assessing and distinguishing the ideal choice, starting with a venture objective and finishing with an exchange.

Characterize your goal, assess the gamble/reward, think about unpredictability, expect occasions, plan a system, and characterize choices boundaries.

Tracking down the Right Option.

We start with the presumption that you have previously recognized a monetary resource — like a stock, product, or ETF — that you wish to exchange utilizing choices. You might have picked this hidden utilizing a stock screener, by utilizing your own examination, or by utilizing outsider exploration. No matter what the strategy for choice, whenever you have distinguished the hidden resource for exchange, there are the six stages for tracking down the best choice:

The six stages understand a coherent point of view that makes it more straightforward to pick a particular choice for exchanging. We should separate what every one of these means includes.

1. Choice Objective.
The beginning stage while making any speculation is your venture goal, and choices exchanging is the same. What goal would you like to accomplish with your choice exchange? Is it to hypothesize a bullish or negative perspective on the fundamental resource? Or on the other hand is it to fence potential drawback gamble on a stock in which you have a huge position?

Might it be said that you are putting on the exchange to procure pay from selling choice charges? For instance, is the methodology part of a covered call against a current stock position or would you say you are composing puts on a stock that you need to claim? Utilizing choices to produce pay is an immeasurably unique methodology contrasted with purchasing choices to guess or to support.

Your initial step is to plan what the goal of the exchange is, on the grounds that it frames the establishment for the resulting steps.

2. Risk/Reward.
The following stage is to decide your gamble reward result, which ought to be subject to your gamble resilience or hunger for risk. On the off chance that you are a moderate financial backer or broker, forceful techniques like composing puts or purchasing a lot of profound out of the cash (OTM) choices may not be fit to you. Each choice technique has a distinct gamble and prize profilc, so ensure you comprehend it completely.

3. Actually look at the Volatility.
Suggested unpredictability is one of the main determinants of a choice's cost, so understand the degree of inferred instability for the choices you are thinking about. Contrast the degree of suggested unpredictability and the stock's verifiable unpredictability and the degree of unpredictability in the expansive market, since

this will be a critical consideration distinguishing your choice exchange/system.

Suggested unpredictability tells you whether different brokers are anticipating that the stock should move a great deal or not. High inferred unpredictability will push up charges, making composing a choice more appealing, accepting the dealer figures instability won't continue to build (which could expand the opportunity of the choice being worked out). Low suggested unpredictability implies less expensive choice charges, which is great for purchasing choices in the event that a dealer expects the hidden stock will move to the point of expanding the worth of the choices.

4. Distinguish Events.
Occasions can be characterized into two general classifications: broad and stock-explicit. Vast occasions are those that influence the wide business sectors, for example, Federal Reserve declarations and monetary information discharges. Stock-explicit occasions are things like profit reports, item dispatches, and side projects.

An occasion can essentially affect suggested instability before its genuine event, and the occasion can colossally affect the stock cost when it happens. So would you like to exploit the flood in unpredictability before a key occasion, or could you rather look out for the sidelines until things settle down?

Recognizing occasions that might affect the fundamental resource can assist you with settling on the fitting time period and termination date for your choice exchange.

5. Devise a Strategy.
In light of the examination led in the past advances, you currently know your speculation unbiased, wanted risk-reward result, level of suggested and verifiable unpredictability, and key occasions that might influence the basic resource. Going through the four stages makes it a lot more straightforward to distinguish a particular choice procedure.

For instance, suppose you are a moderate financial backer with a sizable stock portfolio and need to procure premium pay before organizations begin revealing their quarterly profit in several months. You may, thusly, select a covered call composing methodology, which includes composing approaches to some or every one of the stocks in your portfolio.

As another model, assuming that you are a forceful financial backer who loves remote chances and is persuaded that the business sectors are set out toward a major downfall in something like a half year, you might choose to purchase puts on significant stock files.

6. Lay out Parameters
Since you have recognized the particular choice technique you need to carry out, all that remains is to lay out choice boundaries like termination dates, strike costs, and choice deltas. For instance, you might need to purchase a call with the longest conceivable termination yet at the most minimal conceivable expense, in which case an out-of-the-cash call might be reasonable. On the other hand, on the off chance that you want

a call with a high delta, you might favor an in-the-cash choice.

Chapter 13

PLAY OUT   A   PAIRED   COMPARISON
ANALYSIS.

What is the Paired Comparison Method?
Matched Comparison Method is a helpful
instrument for navigation; it depicts values and
looks at them to one another. It's frequently
hard to pick the most ideal choice when you
have various ones that are far separated.

Every one of the potential choices are thought
about outwardly, prompting an outline that
quickly shows the ideal choice. This makes it
conceivable to look at the overall significance of
restricting rules in a straightforward manner.

On the off chance that there is no genuine
information accessible for pursuing the choice,
the Paired Comparison Method can be an
extremely convenient device. This technique is
otherwise   called   the   Paired   Comparison
Method and Pairwise Comparison.

Needs

Matched Comparison Method can be utilized in various circumstances. For instance, when it's muddled which needs are significant or when assessment models are abstract in nature.

The Paired Comparison Analysis likewise helps when potential choices are rivaling one another, in light of the fact that the best arrangement will be picked eventually. It's simpler to lay out boundaries when there are no clashing prerequisites.

To apply the Paired Comparison Method, utilizing an enormous piece of paper or a flip chart is shrewd. Follow the means under individually for the investigation to work best.

Stage 1: Creating table
Cause a table with lines and sections and finish up the choices that will be contrasted with each other in the primary column and the main segment (the headers of the lines and segments). The vacant cells will remain void until further notice. Assuming there are 4 choices, there are 4 lines and 4 segments and 16

cells; when there are 3 choices, you get 3 columns and 3 sections and 9 cells, etcetera.

Stage 2: Assigning letters

Each choice is presently relegated to a letter (A, B, C etcetera). The choices are referenced in the headers of the lines and segments and every now has a letter so the choices can be appropriately contrasted with one another.

Stage 3: Blocking cells

It's critical to shut out the cells in the table in which similar choices cross-over. Cells that contain a correlation that has been shown before in the table likewise must be shut out. Each correlation ought to just be made once.

Stage 4: Comparing choices

The cells that are left will presently contrast the choices in the lines with the choices in the segments. The letter of the main choice will be noted. For instance, when An is contrasted with C and C is a more significant choice, a C will be recorded in that cell.

Stage 5: Rating choices

The distinction in significance will presently get a rating that will go, for instance, from 0 (no distinction) to 3 (significant contrast).

Stage 6: Listing results
The outcomes are currently united by adding all qualities for every one of the choices being referred to. On the off chance that vital, these sums can be changed over completely to rates.

Matched Comparison by and by
To explain the manner in which a Paired Comparison Method works, here is a model.

Take a business organization that needs to go with a decision between three different Customer Relation Management (CRM) frameworks.

The principal choice is a CRM framework by a prestigious brand, the subsequent choice is a CRM framework that is associated with a cloud administration and the third choice is a CRM framework that comprises different modules. These choices are doled out a letter and are placed in the headers of lines and segments.

In sync 3, a couple of cells are hindered and in this model, 4 cells stay open (see model).

Filling in the scores
The table is currently fit to be filled in. We have picked a scoring arrangement of 0-3. Each choice is thought about, after which the triumphant choice will turn out to be clear. An is contrasted with B, B to C, and C to A.

In the principal examination, An ends up being a higher priority than B, so the letter An is recorded in the open cell. In the subsequent examination, C ends up being a higher priority than B, so the letter C is recorded in the open cell. The last examination is A to C, and An is likewise more significant here. That implies the letter An is recorded in the open cell.

Presently we check significance out. In the event that A will be significantly more significant than B, we put a 3 after A. In the event that An is not really significant contrasted with C, it will get a score of 1. At long last, choice C is of medium significance contrasted with B and subsequently scores a 2.

Matched Comparison Method -
Choice A - working with an eminent CRM framework - is plainly the champ. The rate is a basic computation of the portion of focuses contrasted with the aggregate sum of focuses accessible. The most ideal choice is in a split second clarified by this examination. We really do have to think about this as an instrument, and it ought not to be the best way to pursue a choice. Assuming it just so happens, working with the Modules CRM (C) is liked by the greater part of the organization, that can unquestionably be an ultimate conclusion.

Chapter 14

ALLOW YOUR PERSONAL VALUES TO LEAD
THE WAY.

Five Ways Defining Your Personal Values Will
Lead You To Success

In regular day to day existence we will generally utilize the term esteems rather freely. For the most part, we mean something that is of significance here and there. Frequently there is a moral or normal practice that raises a few qualities over the other in significance. However, in the event that they tell the truth, there is a decent opportunity we don't exactly carry on with our lives in understanding these qualities. What we don't understand is that we have an alternate arrangement of values, values we may not know about, that cause inner turmoil and hinder our prosperity.

Such an easygoing way to deal with grasping our very own qualities, nonetheless, brings about clashing needs, activities and convictions, all of which impede your prosperity. To be a successful person, you should be filling in as really and proficiently as you call constantly. And keeping in mind that there are many devices, tips, and deceives you can utilize, the most crucial is getting clear on what your own fundamental beliefs are.

What happens when your qualities are obvious to you? The outcomes can be shocking and work after some time. They include:

1. Quick Decision Making:
At the point when you know what's vital to you, you understand what move to initiate and what decisions to make. Not an obvious explanation to struggle.

2. Expanding Self-Confidence:
At the point when you understand what you stand you never again dread the judgment of others.

3. Expanding Productivity:
You are inspired like never before to accomplish your objectives. Interruptions

disappear on the grounds that they aren't lined up with your needs.

4. Lessening Conflict and Improving Relationships:
For all intents and purposes all contention is tied in with contending values. At the point when you comprehend your qualities, you understand what you are battling for. You can verbalize that. You can likewise attempt to grasp the other individual's qualities and afterward settle on something worth agreeing on.

5. Building Your Brand:
Clear qualities are brand distinguishers. They become significantly more remarkable when you are experiencing those qualities and it is simple so that everybody might be able to see.

Reward point:
At the point when you know and experience your qualities you make an upright pattern of support. It gets more straightforward and easier for you to adjust and live with those qualities AND you begin getting input and consolation

from others about those qualities and the daily routine you are experiencing.

The most effective method to Get Clear on Your Values

While working with individuals to get clear on their qualities we start with basically posting what you think your qualities are at this moment. Make your rundown of around 10 qualities and the position requests them.

When you have your rundown of values, compose a meaning of each. Take some time and make as itemized a definition as you can about what you explicitly mean by that worth. This isn't the ideal opportunity for a 5-word definition. Be as clear as possible without stressing over being great. Whether it is two or three sentences or a section, this is only for you with the goal that you are clear about what you mean.

As of now you might be seeing that a portion of your qualities are something very similar or rather comparative. Check whether you can unite them. Pick which word and which definition impacts you the most and refine the definition. Right now you may likewise see that a few qualities aren't exactly that vital to you and you can drop them. Others may be surprisingly significant. Drop the immaterial ones, erework the request so your top worth, the worth you would pick assuming that two were going up against one another, is at the top.

Survey your qualities every morning as an update for how you need to act and pick during the day. At night, audit your day and assess how you did. Did you settle on decisions that contention with your qualities? Assuming this is the case, for what reason did you do that? Is there a more significant benefit having an effect on everything?

In the event that you conclude you could do without your qualities, say you are picking solace over achievement, you can transform them. You simply need to begin living as per the new qualities. Throughout the span of months in the event that you truly live as per the new worth it will turn out to be natural to you.

Best of luck!